BUILDING SETS OF TEN

Minta Berry

Crabtree Publishing Company
www.crabtreebooks.com

Author: Minta Berry
Editor: Reagan Miller
Proofreader: Crystal Sikkens
Cover design: Margaret Amy Salter
Editorial director: Kathy Middleton
Production coordinator: Margaret Amy Salter
Prepress technician: Ken Wright
Print coordinator: Katherine Berti
Project manager: Kirsten Holm, Shivi Sharma (Planman
    Technologies)
Photo research: Iti Shrotriya (Planman Technologies)
Technical art: Arka Roy Chaudhary (Planman Technologies)

Photographs:
Cover: Olgysha/Dreamstime; (t) Dani Simmonds/Shutterstock;
(b) Mahesh Patil/Shutterstock; P5: (bkgd.jacks) Juliet
Kaye/Shutterstock, (fgd.fist) Design56 I Dreamstime.com; P6: (t)
Olga Popova/Shutterstock; (b) Elnur/Shutterstock; P7: (t) Olga
Popova/Shutterstock; (c) Elnur/Shutterstock; (b) SunnyS/
Shutterstock; P8: Anna Merzlyakova/Shutterstock; P9: (tl) Galayko
Sergey/Shutterstock; (tr) Galayko Sergey/Shutterstock; (bl)
Galayko Sergey/Shutterstock; (br) Galayko Sergey/Shutterstock;
P10: (bkgd.notebook) Kak2s/Shutterstock, (fgd.cat) Artem
Kursin/Shutterstock, (fgd.dog) Waldemar Dabrowski/Shutterstock;
P11: (t.bkgd.poster) Jorge Pedro Barradas de Casais/Shutterstock,
(t.fgd.basketballplayers) (tl) ArenaCreative/BigStock, (tc)
Alexander Raths I Dreamstime.com, (tr) Yuri Arcurs/BigStock, (bl)
Jupiterimages, Brand X Pictures/Thinkstock, (br) Jupiterimages,
Brand X Pictures/Thinkstock, (t.fgd.baseball players) (tl)
Nickp37/BigStock, (tr) Donald Miralle/Thinkstock, (bl)
Uafotophan/BigStock, (bc) Nicholas Piccillo/Fotolia, (br)
Pudding/BigStock; (b.train) Ojenny/Shutterstock, (b.base ball) MC
PP/Shutterstock; P13: (bkgd.paper) Jackiso/Shutterstock,
(fgd.pencils) Piligrim/Shutterstock; P15: (bkgd.paper) Anusorn P
Nachol/Shutterstock; P18: (base ball) MC_PP/Shutterstock, (tennis
ball) Fotoline/Shutterstock; P19: Fotoline/Shutterstock; P20:
Dja65/Shutterstock; P21: (carrot) Alex Smith/Shutterstock,
(tomato) Top Seller/Shutterstock, (yoghurt) Marc
Dietrich/Shutterstock, (cookie) Piyato/Shutterstock, (orange)
Stefan Fierros/Shutterstock.

t = top, b = bottom, l = left, c= center, r = right, bkgd = background,
fgd = foreground, tr = top right, tl = top left, br = bottom right,
bl = bottom left, tc = top center

Library and Archives Canada Cataloguing in Publication

Berry, Minta
    Building sets of ten / Minta Berry.

(My path to math)
Includes index.
Issued also in electronic formats.
ISBN 978-0-7787-5277-6 (bound).--ISBN 978-0-7787-5266-0 (pbk.)

    1. Set theory--Juvenile literature. I. Title. II. Series: My path to math.

QA248.B47 2011   j511.3'22   C2011-906800-1

Library of Congress Cataloging-in-Publication Data

Berry, Minta.
    Building sets of ten / Minta Berry.
        p. cm. -- (My path to math)
    Includes index.
    ISBN 978-0-7787-5277-6 (reinforced library binding : alk. paper) -- ISBN 978-
0-7787-5266-0 (pbk. : alk. paper) -- ISBN 978-1-4271-8807-6 (electronic pdf) --
ISBN 978-1-4271-9648-4 (electronic html)
    1. Counting--Juvenile literature. 2. Addition--Juvenile literature. 3. Group
theory--Juvenile literature. I. Title.

QA113.B474 2012
513.2'11--dc23

                                            2011040401

Crabtree Publishing Company
www.crabtreebooks.com   1-800-387-7650

Printed in the U.S.A./112011/JA20111018

Published in Canada
Crabtree Publishing
616 Welland Ave.
St. Catharines, ON
L2M 5V6

Published in the United States
Crabtree Publishing
PMB 59051
350 Fifth Avenue, 59th Floor
New York, New York 10118

Published in the United Kingdom
Crabtree Publishing
Maritime House
Basin Road North, Hove
BN41 1WR

Published in Australia
Crabtree Publishing
3 Charles Street
Coburg North
VIC 3058

Contents

Basic Counting

Aakar and Miranda visit Grandma Sundara. They have lunch together. After lunch, Grandma helps them play a game. She gives them ten jacks.

Miranda lines up the jacks. Help **count** the jacks.

Miranda and Aakar count ten jacks. Grandma Sundara gives them the ball they will need to play the game.

Activity Box

Look at the balls in the table.
How many balls are red?
How many are green?
How many are blue?

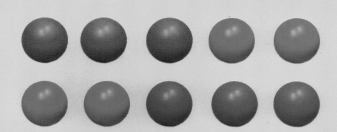

Aakar tosses the ball in the air. He takes one jack and catches the ball. Count the jacks still on the table. There are now nine jacks.

5

Ways to Ten

Miranda and Aakar go shopping with Grandma. She asks both children to choose ten pears.

Miranda gets six red pears and four yellow pears.

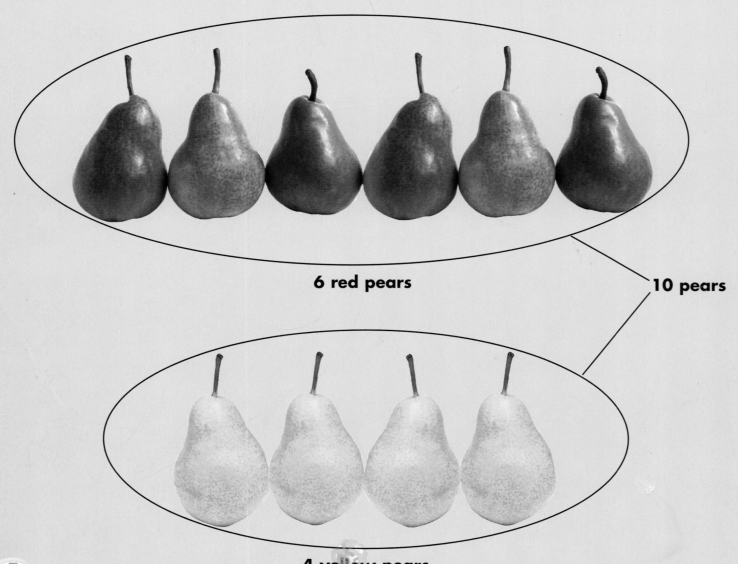

6 red pears

10 pears

4 yellow pears

Aakar gets three red pears and seven yellow pears.

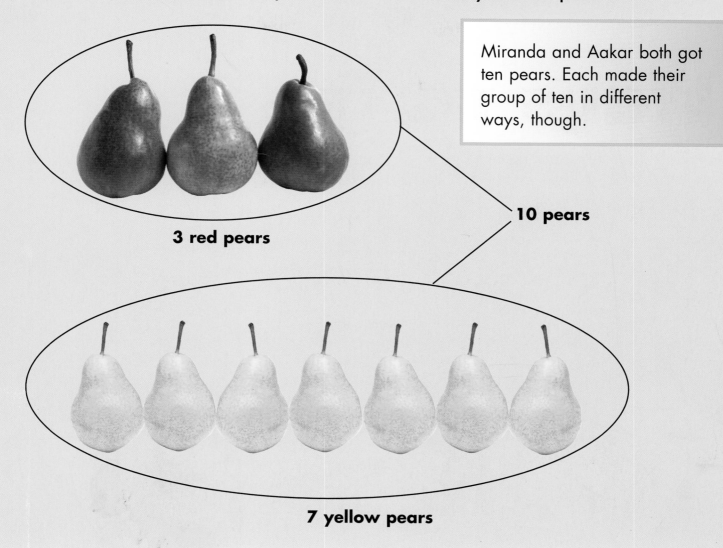

Miranda and Aakar both got ten pears. Each made their group of ten in different ways, though.

10 pears

3 red pears

7 yellow pears

Activity Box

Look at the glasses of milk.

How many glasses are filled with white milk?

How many glasses are filled with chocolate milk?

How many glasses of milk are there?

Making a Number Sentence

Grandma shares a game with Aakar. She gives him ten beans. One side of the bean is painted. One side is plain. She puts the beans in a bag. Aakar shakes the bag and spills the beans on the table.

Count the painted beans. Then count the plain beans. Next count all the beans.

Painted Beans	Plain Beans	Total Beans
6	4	10

Grandma writes a **number sentence** on a piece of paper. It shows that six plus four equals ten. The **+** sign means to **add** two things.

$$6 + 4 = 10$$

Aakar shows Miranda the bean adding game Grandma Sundara taught him. They take turns spilling the beans four times. They write down the results. Then they write number sentences that show their results.

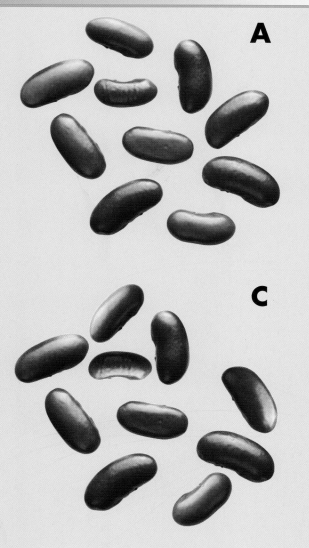

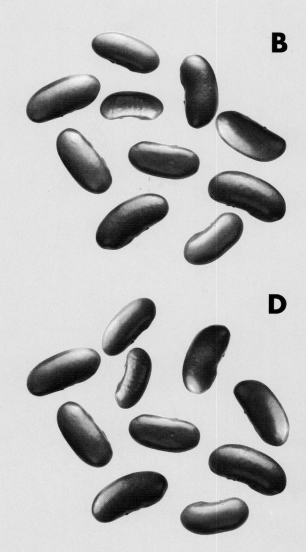

Spill	Painted Beans	Plain Beans	Total Beans
A	2	8	10
B	9	1	10
C	5	5	10
D	4	6	10

Number Sentences

$2 + 8 = 10$

$9 + 1 = 10$

$5 + 5 = 10$

$4 + 6 = 10$

9

Addition Pictures

Miranda is decorating her notebook with stickers. She finds ten stickers of dogs and cats.

Eight of the stickers are of dogs. Two of the stickers are of cats. She puts the stickers on the cover of her notebook.

She adds the dogs and cats. What number sentence shows the number of dogs and the number of cats?

$$8 + 2 = 10$$

Aakar likes baseball. He also likes basketball. He finds ten pictures of his favorite players. He makes a poster for his bedroom with the pictures. Then Aakar

writes a number sentence that matches the pictures on his poster. What number sentence did he write?

Activity Box

Look at these pictures. Write a number sentence to show the total number of objects.

Write your own number sentence. Then draw a picture to show what the number sentence means.

Seeing a Pattern

Grandma shows Aakar a chart. It shows all of the ways to add to ten.

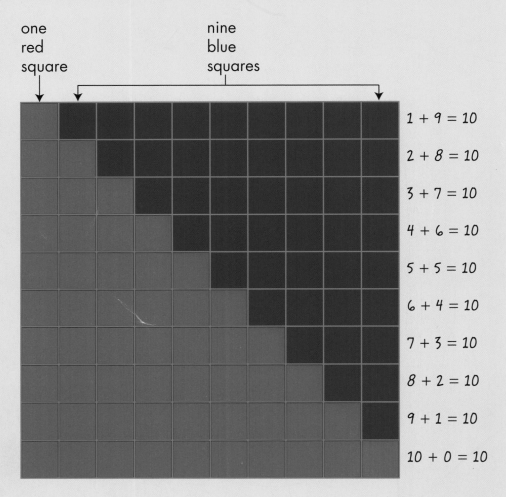

one red square

nine blue squares

$1 + 9 = 10$

$2 + 8 = 10$

$3 + 7 = 10$

$4 + 6 = 10$

$5 + 5 = 10$

$6 + 4 = 10$

$7 + 3 = 10$

$8 + 2 = 10$

$9 + 1 = 10$

$10 + 0 = 10$

There are ten squares in each line of the chart. Aakar counts each colored square. Grandma writes the number sentence. Each number sentence shows the number of red and blue squares that make up a line of ten.

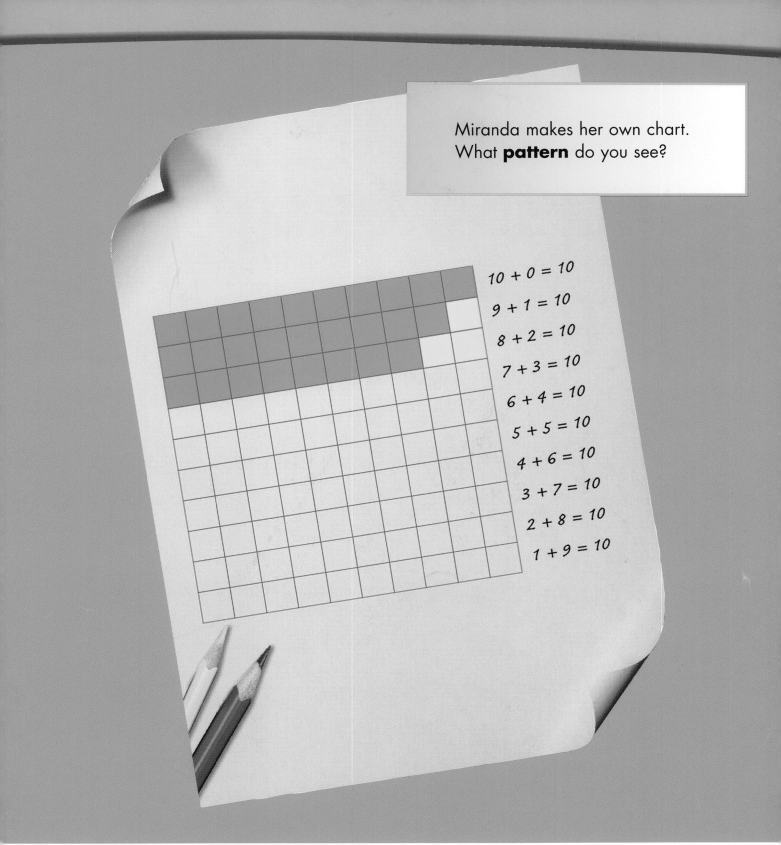

Miranda makes her own chart.
What **pattern** do you see?

10 + 0 = 10
9 + 1 = 10
8 + 2 = 10
7 + 3 = 10
6 + 4 = 10
5 + 5 = 10
4 + 6 = 10
3 + 7 = 10
2 + 8 = 10
1 + 9 = 10

Activity Box

Miranda has a new pencil case that holds
ten pencils. She puts seven pencils in the pencil
case. Use the chart above to find how many
more pencils will fit in her pencil case.

Summing It Up

Aakar sees a pattern to adding to ten. Look at the two number sentences.

$$4 + 6 = 10$$
$$6 + 4 = 10$$

What do you see? Four plus six equals ten.
And six plus four equals ten.

Does this pattern work with other numbers?

$$7 + 3 = 10$$
$$3 + 7 = 10$$

Yes. Seven plus three equals ten.
And three plus seven equals ten.

Activity Box

Look at the number sentences. What number is missing?
You can use blocks or counters to help you.

$1 + ? = 10$ $? + 6 = 10$ $5 + ? = 10$ $10 + ? = 10$

$$\begin{array}{r} 3 \\ + \ ? \\ \hline 10 \end{array} \qquad \begin{array}{r} ? \\ + 2 \\ \hline 10 \end{array} \qquad \begin{array}{r} 9 \\ + \ ? \\ \hline 10 \end{array}$$

Number sentences mean the same whether they are written up and down or across.

$4 + ? = 10$ $? + 5 = 10$ $7 + ? = 10$

$$\begin{array}{r} 9 \\ +\ ? \\ \hline 10 \end{array}$$ $$\begin{array}{r} ? \\ +\ 6 \\ \hline 10 \end{array}$$ $$\begin{array}{r} 0 \\ +\ ? \\ \hline 10 \end{array}$$

$8 + ? = 10$ $? + 1 = 10$ $3 + ? = 10$

$$\begin{array}{r} 1 \\ +\ ? \\ \hline 10 \end{array}$$ $$\begin{array}{r} ? \\ +\ 5 \\ \hline 10 \end{array}$$ $$\begin{array}{r} 2 \\ +\ ? \\ \hline 10 \end{array}$$

Grandma Sundara writes number sentences on a paper. Aakar and Miranda take turns telling her the answers.

Three Things Make Ten

Grandma Sundara finds a deck of cards. She puts three cards on the table. Aakar counts the **symbols** on the cards.

2   5   3

Aakar writes a number sentence for the cards.

2 + 5 + 3 = 10

Aakar sees that three numbers can be added to make ten.

Activity Box

Look at the cards. Write number sentences to match each set of three cards.

There are many ways to
add to ten.

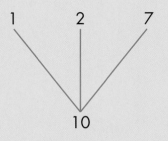

1   2   7

10

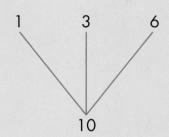

1   3   6

10

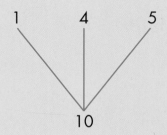

1   4   5

10

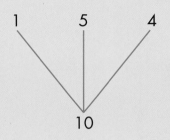

1   5   4

10

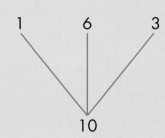

1   6   3

10

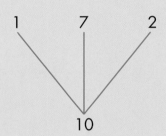

1   7   2

10

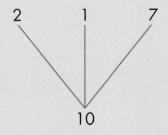

2   1   7

10

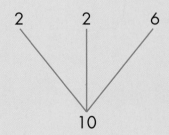

2   2   6

10

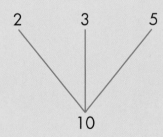

2   3   5

10

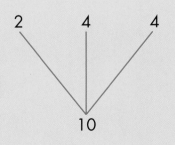

2   4   4

10

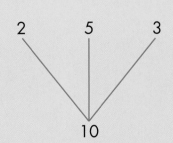

2   5   3

10

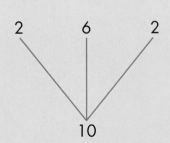

2   6   2

10

Checking Your Work

Grandma Sundara shows Aakar and Miranda how to check their work. They used addition to solve the problems. She tells them they can use subtraction to make sure they found the right answers.

She writes two number sentences for them. One number sentence uses addition. Then she turns the sentence around. She uses the same numbers to create a number sentence that uses **subtraction**.
The numbers in the two number sentences are related. They are part of a **fact family**.

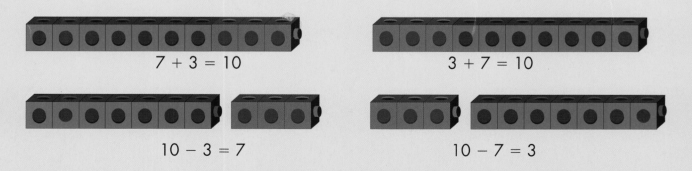

7 + 3 = 10   3 + 7 = 10

10 − 3 = 7   10 − 7 = 3

The numbers 3, 7, and 10 make a fact family.

Grandma Sundara puts ten baseballs and tennis balls on the table.

She asks Miranda to write a number sentence about the balls. Miranda writes this number sentence:

6 + 4 = 10

Is Miranda right?

Then Grandma Sundara asks Miranda to take away the baseballs.

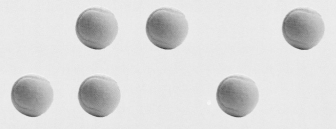

She asks Aakar to write the number sentence that tells what Miranda just did. This number sentence will use subtraction. Aakar writes:

10 – 4 = 6

Is Aakar right?

Activity Box

Look at these number sentences that use addition. Then write the number sentence that uses subtraction to check the solution. The first one is done for you.

2 + 8 = 10	10 – 8 = 2
5 + 5 = 10	
1 + 9 = 10	

What is Missing from Ten?

Grandma Sundara bought ten juice boxes. Now there are seven juice boxes. How many are missing?

Aakar knows the number of juice boxes she bought and the number of juice boxes that are left. He uses these numbers to write a number sentence.

$$10 = 7 + ?$$

What number plus seven makes ten? Miranda completes the number sentence.

$$10 = 7 + 3$$

Activity Box

Choose ten crayons. Put the crayons in two groups. Then write the number sentence to show your groups.

$$10 = \ ? \ + \ ?$$

Make two new groups with the crayons. Write the number sentence to show your new groups.

20

Aakar chooses items from Grandma's kitchen. He and Miranda use the objects to make ten.

10

? + ?

10

? + ? + ?

Aakar uses snacks to make ten items. He asks Miranda to fill in the missing number to complete the number sentences.

Glossary

+ The math symbol that means to add

− The math symbol that means to subtract

add Putting two units or things together

count Naming numbers in order
(1, 2, 3, 4, 5, 6, and so on)

fact family A group of addition and subtraction number sentences that are related

number sentence A math sentence using numbers (1, 2, 3) and symbols (+, =)

pattern A set of things that follows a rule

subtraction Taking one number away from another number

symbol A design or image

Math Facts Chant for Ten

Make a ten. Make a ten.

We know ways to make a ten.

9 + 1 and 8 + 2;

They both equal ten. It's true.

7 + 3 and 6 + 4;

Do you know there are two more?

5 + 5 and 0 + 10;

Now let's say them all again!

Index